Answers from the Quiet

Advice for Living Well

Barbara Waggoner

Presentation by *BookLeaf Publishing*

Web: www.bookleafpub.com

E-mail: info@bookleafpub.com

ISBN: 9789357445160

First edition 2022

DEDICATION

I dedicate this book to all the troubles, setbacks, hardships, losses, betrayals, fears, disappointments and tears that have graced my life. And the people who have helped me through them. These "negative" things have provided a dedicated motivation within me to find answers — answers that work. And the energy to try them out.

I equally dedicate it to the miraculous synchronicities that have occurred with such beauty that I couldn't miss seeing them, and to stand in awe of the incredible choreography that had to occur to bring them forth. They have taught me to see and hear beyond the obvious.

And I dedicate this to my sons, and grandsons who have provided for me the greatest experience of love that life has to offer: Eric and John, and their sons, Cameron, Nicholas and Nolan who carry the Waggoner name and their amazingly intense brilliance. And to my beautiful daughters-in-law Cristina, Carolyn and Llsa, mothers and women extrordinare who show me the true meaning of loving motherhood!

ACKNOWLEDGEMENT

Forever thanks to Cathy Drew, the beautiful being who shared the idea of listening for guidance, and has continued to teach and encourage me throughout the years. And total gratitude to my lifelong friends Carol Toone who sent me the "21 Day Poetry Challenge" which resulted in publishing this book, and awesome Jill Kennedy and Cathy Drew who brainstormed with me the selection and refinement of what you read inside.

And much acknowledgement is owed to the many marvelous teachers who have enriched my life and my thoughts. Most especially to Esther Hicks/Abraham, John Grinder and Richard Bandler and Genie LaBorde for my life transforming Neuro Linguistic Programming training, Michael Singer, Byron Katie, HeartMath Institute and so many others who have moved me and educated me deeply!!

PREFACE

These poems are in a way "delivered" to me. Usually as an answer to a worry, question or problem I am experiencing. I ask a question and then I simply wait until an answer begins out of the quiet.

 The stanzas herein come in an interesting way. After I ask a question and listen, I hear (or think--not sure which. It is subtle.) half a line and write it down and then I hear and record the rest of the line. It comes forth in rhythm and rhyme. So ultimately, then, at the end we have a poem. And then I get the gift of reading it to see what message it holds. I am often charmed and awed by what I read, (and sometimes I need a dictionary.) So these poems are personal guidance for me, and my hope is there is something of value for you, also.

It all began long ago when I was visiting a friend, Cathy Drew, who has a practice of awakening in the morning and listening for and transcribing guidance for herself. I decided to try it also on this trip. I awoke around 3 am, and since I was awake, I did as she does and

listened.   I wrote down what seemed to be
gibberish nonsense, and fell back asleep. But it
came in rhythm and rhyme, so that was fun.
Reading it in the morning, we both discovered
it made a lot of sense.

Now, over the years, it is so consistently there
for me, I have come to trust and rely on it. This
little book, however, is my first pathway for
publicly sharing it. Welcome to my world of
advice through rhythm and rhyme. From the
Quiet.

UPS & DOWNS

When clouds are around, the sun is not gone.
In the deepest night, daybreak is coming on
As surely as things happen to throw you off
stride
Infinite goodness will walk by your side.

Don't be put off by the surf warnings in your
life
Think of them like a surfer's delight.
Determine to ride them with balance and poise
With minute adjustments that quiet the noise.

Ups and Downs are not a bad thing
Have you ever seen kids on a trampoline?
You have choice in how you take these
continuous swings
Are you beaten down or rather given wings?

Stay in balance when your "up" turns to
"down"
You'll always discover a way to rebound
Knowing this, you can relax and play...
Infinite goodness is always showing you the
way.

CRITICISM

You think it's a virtue to notice where you fall
short
But you have no idea how this will abort –
All that is good that is lined up — heading your
way
The critique stops the flow and takes miracles
out of play.

Notice what happens when criticism stops
Your essential nature surfaces, unaided, to the
top
Love and acceptance join their way in
By simply stopping critique – appreciation rolls
in.

Gently soothe yourself when your efforts fall
flat
Love your mistakes, broken promises, wrinkles,
and fat
Smile when bad habits win one more time
Love all your humanness and know it's all fine.

Acceptance and love are the antidote to all —
Healing the energy and allowing the call
to open the pathway to all that is good
Amusement is the power: be that understood.

REVERENCE

There is only right now in any day
Given to you to squander or to play
Each day is a gift to create what you will
You might want to be thoughtful about how you
fill.

Look outside for the wonders that are there
Appreciate the comfort of your blessed favorite
chair
Swoon with the taste of what you choose to eat
And count the many blessings of the people who
you meet.

Being in the moment and in your body too
Give you confirmation of what you know is true
Life is exquisite and offers continuous joys
Pamper your body and quiet mental noise.

Choose to spend this day in a small experiment
With joy and connection, leave that fingerprint
Do each task with reverence and exalted attitude
And see the wondrous magic with which they are
imbued.

Definition of REVERENCE: high regard, great respect, acclaim, admiration, appreciation, favor.

OVERWHELM

See how much you can get done this day
The sense of completion will lighten your way
Tackle a big project and whittle it down
Do the broad strokes and don't get bogged down.

Overwhelm tells you "You're not enough."
"You don't know where to start to handle this
stuff."
But you are the captain at the helm
Make decisions easily to banish overwhelm.

You can't make a mistake because it's never quite
over
One decision will lead to another
If you don't like the outcome of a decision you've
made
Make another to equalize the trade.

Most of all, make each project fun
Enjoy the process and the sum
You'll enjoy great aliveness when you finish this
way
So make it part of the process along the way.

Jump right in and don't put off!
With wisdom flowing and criticism lost
You can't imagine how much you can accomplish
today
When you get really excited and approach it as
play.

WHAT YOUR BODY WANTS

Let's talk about what your body would like to
be
What tunes it up and what sets it free…
Exuberance, enthusiasm and authenticity
Are miracle workers for your chemistry.

They're all cut from the same map, you see
Different iterations of the same tapestry
A wonderful symphony of billions of cells
Doing their part as aliveness swells.

Exuberance adds energy and far-reaching
cooperation
So your internal workings move smoothly with
precision
The billions of processes can hum along nicely
And all that is needed is given precisely.

Enthusiasm, Authenticity, and Exuberance
Are a wonderful elixir which call cells to dance
And gives all your intentions a fertile chance—

Creating energy to spare that is not
happenstance.

It's like a new car with horsepower to spare
That can happily take you anywhere
The thread of aliveness that brought you to
Earth
Do feel that feeling, as you provide worth.

PRESENCE

Behold another day to make special and fine
Pay no attention to what is behind
Make this day as special as can be
By moving into joy from what you can see.

Little moments of presence are ultimately the key
Bringing your whole self, right where you be
Attending to what's there right here and right now
Will bring peace and certainty — this is the "how."

Your scattered awareness of your "must" and your "should"
Diminish your power to do what you could
Start with the small things until you understand the power
Filling a "minute" fully as if it were an hour.

You can't go back or dictate your future
This is the moment to select to have pleasure
And that, my dear, is a mental ability
That has nothing to do with what seems like reality.

HIDDEN MEANING

Words with power are imbued
Saying them create a mood
They carry an expectation that is hidden
But we respond to it as if it is bidden...

If I say "I would" then I might or I could
If I say "I could" possibilities unfurl
If I say "I should" I definitely won't
If I say "I won't" I most probably will
If I say "I will" it's sure, either future or now
If I say "I can" I'm filled with promise
If I say "I get to" I'm filled with excitement
If I say "I have to" dread descends
If I say "I can't" my abilities end
If I say "I don't" I'm locked in stone
If I say "I didn't" I rewrite history and predict
my future
If I say "I get to" I'm ready to go
So here's to "get to" the Merlin of "Go."

ALIGNMENT

Posture is something to think about today,
A lifetime of habits cause everything to stay
Just about the same with hunching and scrunching
While your body is much happier with rolling and
stretching.

How you sit is something to attend
"Computer-Sitting" causes an unhealthy bend
Keeping your head balanced up over your
shoulders
Makes for free-flowing energy and a mood that is
bolder.

You well know the S-Curve is right for your back
But you might not know the repercussions from
the lack —
Hampered energy, digestion, joint freedom and
more
Are the gifts that poor posture has in store.

Let your head rock gently and notice the great
weight
Think of the mischief slight off-balance can create
Place your head this day in the neutral-weight zone

And the rest of your posture will follow along

Your shoulders fall back and your lungs release
The curve in your back will easily increase
Grounded in your pelvis your energy flows
And fluidity in walking eases and grows.

Notice your mood with a head that's "on straight"
And feel the enthusiasm right out of the gate
Banish your lifetime of sitting a certain way
And feel the new body that posture can parlay.

THE GIFT

Out of a crisis comes first a storm
Anger at the situation that disturbs the norm
But peace and solution come from a decision to
transcend
To welcome it in and make it a friend.

Every dark cloud has gifts to bestow
Your work is to let fear and anger go
In the peaceful appreciation of what crisis can
bring
You open the door and allow magic to reign.

Your mind wants to show you what "bad" will
show up
Making sure that defense and fear are ramped
up...
Invent, instead, a game of creation
Where what comes forth will exceed
expectation.

The act of transcending is the decisive key
Allowing really good things to come to be
At first they look terrible, but you'll come to
see

That they've brought great gifts ultimately.

Welcome the "terrible" and make it an
adventure
To expect and notice the profound treasure
When you treat the trouble as a friend there to
help you
You harmonize with all that's good to support
you.

STRONG EMOTION

Stirring of emotion is purposefully divine
Presenting you power, breaking out of time
The focus forces the rupture of ennui
To offer an opening for you to be free.

Your habits enforce repetitive thought strings
Lead you to sameness and away from surprising
things
So strong emotion — whether positive or dark
—

Breaks the habitual, allowing newness a spark.

Strong emotion is the doorway to hidden
opportunity
Providing the power to magnetize synergy
To choose a new way and better your plight
With the urgency you need to re-set and re-lite.

Anger, disappointment and other strong vibing
Lead you to the hidden places that really need
reviving
Add fresh air and fresh thoughts, not what's
gone before
To reawaken the person you love and adore.

IT HAPPENED! NOW WHAT?

When a door slams shut, it gives you finality
It makes going forward an absolute reality
You then can go forward without looking back
So gather your energy to keep you on track.

You so love to stay in your comfort zone
But it's time to branch out and make a new
home
Open to a world that's exciting and new
And see what God has in store for you.

Embrace change because it's a means to an end
Bringing you greater wisdom and new friends
A crisis will mobilize your forces to bear
Giving you powers you didn't know were there.

You came here to live for the fun of it all
So join this adventure for the fun that's on call
Laugh at the ludicrous because it is funny
Let go of the seriousness and know life is sunny

It's not about the resources you have on hand
It's more how you dance with the ultimate plan
Follow your urgings just as they come
Remarkable things await, experience them as
fun

ARGUMENT

It's the thinking that you're right
That fuels motivation for you to fight —
And in the fight this righteousness
Presents your point of view as best.

The other then defends their stance
And hardens their position's dance
And thus neither has the chance
To think it from the other's glance.

And then the issue becomes to win
And produce a loser in the end
Thus two people fight for honor
Instead of seeking solutions to ponder.

The power to win an honorable fight
Is to drop the issue of who is "right"
And explore the way each looks at it
Until good-will can find a fit.

The world is a diverse and wondrous place
And there is always room to find a space
For peaceful existence of two points of view
So that you can win ~ and the other too.

STILLNESS

Stillness is always the best policy
No matter what is going topsy-turvy
Like a stone dropped in water creates a ripple
Your stillness expands outward making things
simple.

Stillness lets go of your irritations
And cancels automatic expectations
Allowing the situation to simply "be"
Which will bring choreography to the mystery.

There is an invisible stream of goodness, you
see
That can come to you when the pathway is free
And stillness clears the path for you
So goodness can find its way to you.

Thus the answer to most problems
Is in stopping the effort to solve them
Find your stillness and let it be there
And watch how concerns vanish into thin air.

Worry won't do it, nor will defense
Your power is in taking the chance
To let everything go and simply be still
And let the stillness bring answers that fulfill.

WORRY

Worrying is your Achilles heel
It's inventing a future that seems to you real
It's just an imagination with catastrophe's
theme
That has you suffering before it's even being

"What bad can happen?" is the hidden refrain
That spins in your mind to drive you insane
It is impossible to try to predict all bad things
And worse, to worry how to solve everything.

"Worry is interest on trouble before it comes
due"
Is what some people have said to you.
It messes with your chemistry, initiative,
motivation,
And puts the wrong aim on your devotion

If inventing a future is your favorite repast
Start with a query with a different ask
Try "What good can happen?" to start your
musing
Which makes you inspired instead of inventing
losing.

It opens you up instead of closing you down
And creates good feelings all around
It invites you to play and be brave and OK
And puts aliveness in your heart and in your
day.

TENSION

When feeling exhausted at the end of the day
Sit comfortably down and do not delay
Concentrate deeply on just letting go
Focus your intention to let silence flow.

A state this complete has recuperative powers
So rest is achieved in minutes not hours
All your will, your commitment, your attention
and intent
Work synchronistically 'til suspension you
invent

Your mind will maneuver to break your
attention
To take flight of fancy or worried distraction
Remind yourself to relax into resting and
floating
Giving each cell its moment of coasting

This foray into nothingness is an amazing elixir
Your weariness dissipates and energy comes
quicker
Some moments like this and you'll be refreshed
and awake

This tiny little sojourn is all it will take.

Your body loves having a soulful director
And is an eager partner when you unite sectors
It will mobilize miracles when you align all
inside
And will bless you with the joy of being alive!

ADVICE FOR DIS-EASE

Illness comes up when emotions spill over
Bubbling inside of a tight-fitting cover
All the little nuisances that pile up through the
day
Feed the illness endlessly unless you find a way
To settle down the molecules — like a deep still
pond
Replacing thoughts of "this ain't right" with
things becoming fond.

Daffodils delight the dawn and daylight does
not sway
The alphabet come hither feel that puts bad
things away
You do not need to change your life but only
put away
Spending time on what is wrong to complain
about today.

Fixate on the things you love from morning
until night

Awakening your awareness of which thoughts
bring delight
Live a long and healthy life as stars do in the
day
True on course and shining through as you find
the way.

The path of health is set out for you with
twinkles highlighting time
You do not need to work very hard, just know
that things are fine
Each pleasant moment is a twinkle in the path
of time
Following one after another will leave your
troubles behind

MY PERSON

The wheels of magnetism for "the one"
Are working for you invisibly done
Lots of action in the world is not really needed
Being your loving self is the step completed.

You have your walls and strong requirements
That cloud the seeing of deep refinements
You miss a lot by a quick dismissal
And you lose the chance for playful rehearsal.

Fascination is your divining rod
To help you see what is beyond
Be open and fascinated with all you meet
And forget it is a partner that you seek

Fascination and openness are a secret door
To reveal to you the inner core
To find a resonance of substance and style
To know if you want to stay awhile

Treat each person as a long-lost friend
Loving to catch up with them again
Create interaction that fulfills you both
So that heart-to-heart joining can come forth.

PLANNING

Planning is a mission of hope
To give certainty so you can cope
It takes the unknown and gives it form
So your future is set and will conform.

But best laid plans can go awry
Placing you back in the unknown – to try
To find your footing and to make it great
And invent new things to initiate.

Planning bring peace to an anxious mind
So you think you know what you will find
But there is another way to live life though
That brings more joy and surprise to you.

Instead of planning how it will be
Set yourself up with an energy tree
The branches unknown, but the feeling is there
And explore what can happen as you travel
there.

Put joy in your heart, your mind, and soul
Then travel around and explore the whole

Follow impressions and hunches that occur to
you
And discover what Life is planning for you.

LAUGHTER

As you walk along your path today
Look for opportunities to laugh and play
Laughing at incongruities that arise
Take away the sting that would be there
otherwise

Laughter works miracles for your inner self
Relieving stress and bringing forth health
A couple of minutes of hilarity
Tune you up like a magic pharmacy

It's even good to laugh for no reason
Perfect therapy for any season
Get it started by deciding to
Then let those chemicals overrun you.

Tune into things that make you laugh
It refreshes you like an inner bath
Like children who laugh and giggle at anything
Bubble into laughter just as your 'thing.'

Laughter is your gift to you
A healthy elixir through and through
Spend this day looking for things that are funny
And discover that joy makes your life sunny.

MAKE LIFE FULFILLING

Fulfillment is the sense that all is well and good
Nothing needs doing and there's nothing to be
understood
You are alright and so is the world
Nothing left but enjoying good feelings
unfurled.

The question is how to muster that frequency
Is it earned or simply given freely?
Is it outside recognition and applause
Or internal appreciation when you take pause?

Or is it something else of a finer distinction…
A bestowed gift at birth and a constant
invitation
To settle yourself back into fulfillment,
Without working, earning or another's
judgement

Fill yourself up with the use of your will
Step into your worthiness and let it fulfill
In that place, everything you do
Fills you with wonder and spirits renew.

FLY FREE

Busy-ness abounds...but peace can be found
In concentrating on "doing" you're going round
and round
An easier course is to go into your inner core
And find that serene place that doesn't want for
more.

This is the place where all things can be
The power to find and guide you to see
A place of safety, adoration, and light
That settles your worries and makes things
right.

You have more power than you can know
To direct and write this picture-show
Act from that place of serenity and grace
And things will coincidentally fall into place.

It's not the "doing" that ultimately is the key
It's finding the serenity that has you fly free
It's knowing you're powerful and lucky as can
be

That has you discover the deliciousness that can
come to be.

So, for today, feel how lucky you are
All that is needed is here — not far
You can take a few risks along the way
Cause you know that you're lucky and luck
runs your way.

Thank you for journeying into "the
quiet"with me!
Barbara Waggoner